A STEP–BY–STEP GUIDE TO

RESTORING & REPAIRING FURNITURE

A STEP–BY–STEP GUIDE TO

RESTORING & REPAIRING FURNITURE

How to give any job the professional touch

Consultant Editor: Alan Smith
Revised and Updated by Chris Jarrey

THUNDER BAY
P·R·E·S·S

Published in the United States by
Thunder Bay Press
5880 Oberlin Drive, Suite 400
San Diego, CA 92121-4794
http://www.advmkt.com

ISBN 1-57145-229-X

QUMSGRF

This book was produced by
Quantum Books Ltd
6 Blundell Street
London N7 9BH

Library of Congress Cataloging-in-Publication
Data available upon request.

1   2 3 4 5 99 00 01 02 03

Reproduced in Singapore by Eray Scan Pte Ltd
Printed and bound in Singapore by Star Standard Industries Pte Ltd

CONTENTS

How to Use This Book

As everybody knows, hiring a professional to restore a piece of damaged furniture to its former glory is expensive – and with a little time and patience you can achieve a very similar result with your own endeavors. This book is designed for enthusiasts who not only want to save money by restoring their own furniture but also seek the satisfaction of knowing they have done it themselves. It is a comprehensive manual directed both at the novice and at the more experienced restorer; it tackles every aspect of furniture restoration from simple cleaning methods to intricate cabinet repairs. This book will equip you with the basic knowledge for comprehensive restoration projects, however, if you are in any doubt I recommend that you consult an expert, inexperienced restoration can greatly devalue antique furniture.

For convenience, the book is divided into three sections: "Woodwork," "Other Materials," and "Upholstery." Each section has a few pages detailing the essential tools and materials relevant to that section, followed by a series of how-to-do-it projects. All the projects are illustrated by detailed photographs and easy-to-follow drawings, which show you exactly what to do.

WOODWORK

This section shows you how to deal with everything from wobbly chair legs to blistered marquetry, how to clean furniture without ruining it, and how to achieve a professional luster when polishing. If you develop a "feeling" for restoring wooden furniture, you will need specialized tools and ultimately a work space in which to use them. Advice on how to set up a workshop is therefore included in this section.

OTHER MATERIALS

This section shows you how to restore all sorts of defects in furniture that is not derived entirely from a tree trunk. Everything from plastic to *papier mâché* and glass is covered. All you need to know about restoring cane and rush furniture - which is both vulnerable and frail – is also contained in this section.

UPHOLSTERY

Upholstery is a world unto its own. There are many ways to make a pillow and many ways to render a soft chair. This section makes it simple and easy to understand. The jargon is explained and the projects cover such things as making pillows and renewing webbing.

GLOSSARY

The glossary at the end of the book gives explanations of some of the technical words and phrases used in the practical sections.

PROFESSIONAL TIPS

All professional cabinetmakers and furniture restorers have their own 'secret' tips, which can save you a considerable amount of time and effort, as well as assist you in the selection of the best tools and equipment for any given job. All the tips included in this book have been provided by successful professional restorers and are the result of their many years of experience in their respective fields. Written in plain language, the tips are included in boxes in the relevant work chapters.

Opposite page
Top left
Cleaning polished wood.
Top right
Stripping old veneer.
Bottom left
Renewing a rush seat.
Bottom right
Making piping for pillows.

This page
Top left
Gilding a shell.
Top right
Repairing a caned seat.
Bottom left
Attaching the covering to a drop-in set.
Bottom right
Making a stitched edge for an overstuffed chair.

Woodwork

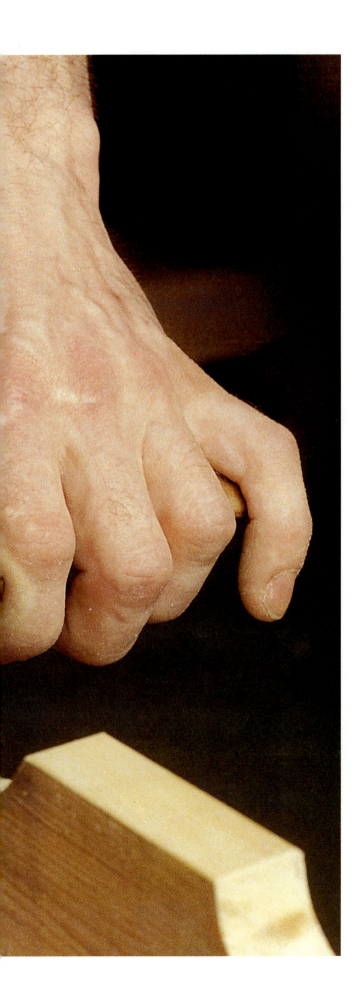

To many people, the words "restoration" and "repair" mean the same thing. There is, however, a subtle difference. Repairing a piece of furniture is to mend it so that it is once more serviceable, without consideration of or respect for its original appearance; restoring a piece, on the other hand, means returning it as nearly as possible to its authentic state whilst preserving as much as possible of the patina of the years.

Examination of a piece of old furniture will usually reveal repair or restoration work undertaken at various intervals throughout its life. Such work is not always immediately apparent: for example, the signs of repair on a veneered surface may be merely subtle variations in grain, texture, or color. And whereas mends to broken legs are easy to detect, leg joints can be put back almost invisibly. In extreme cases, some parts - such as the ball feet of a sideboard - may have been removed altogether.

Successful repair and restoration require special tools. There are numerous types of these, and each type appears in many guises. However, although a professional cabinetmaker will usually possess a great number of specialist tools, the beginner can often do satisfactory work with only a limited number. In addition to the traditional hand tools, you can also use electric power tools which can often make a job quicker and easier. But it is as well to be wary of power tools. They may be quicker but they are not necessarily better, are rarely suitable for precision work, and are potentially dangerous.

Cabinetmakers are usually only too willing to give help and advice, particularly if you catch them out of working hours. It is always worth picking their brains to elicit their "tricks of the trade," to find out how to use special tools, and to discover better ways of using the traditional ones.

Repair and restoration require a patience and skill which improves with experience. A high degree of accuracy and a willingness to become familiar with the technical terms are essential to successful work. Given time, patience, and aptitude, anyone can restore a piece of furniture to its former glory.

Left
Making a new top for a dresser. Shown here:
using a spokeshave to tidy up some rough edges
left by a jigsaw.

Types of Wood

Timber is bought and sold in many different ways, and there are literally thousands of types of wood. To the novice woodworker, buying timber can be confusing, and the jargon used by merchants does not make matters any simpler.

BUYING TIMBER

High-quality furniture is usually constructed from hardwood, whereas lesser-quality pieces are often made from softwood, or even from manmade boards. Softwood is timber from an evergreen tree like a pine or a spruce. These trees grow comparatively quickly, and consequently their timber is not very dense. Hardwood is timber from a deciduous tree. These trees tend to grow slowly, and consequently their wood is hard, dense, and heavy. (Just to confuse matters, balsa is classified as a hardwood even though its timber is light and soft.) Oak, mahogany, teak, and walnut are all hardwoods that are commonly used in the construction of furniture. Hardwoods must be seasoned before they are used. Some hardwoods take many years to season thoroughly, and this, of course, adds to the expense of buying them. Hardwood is usually sold rough-sawn in the form of planks or blocks. Of the many manmade boards used to make furniture, plywood, blockboard, MDF, and chipboard are the most common. Chipboard, the weakest of the three, is often coated with a layer of melamine or a plastic laminate.

TIMBER MOLDINGS

Moldings (or beading, as they are sometimes called) are sold in a plethora of different profiles, but it is not always easy to find an exact match for an existing piece –

1 Cherry
2 Cedar
3 Ash
4 Holly
5 Pine
6 Beech
7 Pear
8 Canadian birch
9 Boxwood
10 Chestnut
11 Mahogany
12 Sycamore
13 Lime
14 Maple
15 Walnut
16 Elm
17 Oak
18 Yew

particularly if it is old. This can be very frustrating if you are trying to patch a piece of furniture! If the worst comes to the worst, you may have to commission a timber yard to cut a molding especially for you. Alternatively, you could shape a length of wood yourself, using a specially shaped plane. When buying moldings, check that they are straight and that they are free of knots. Knots have the habit of falling out or "weeping" unless they are treated with a knotting compound first. Moldings can be of either softwood or hardwood, but hardwood ranges are limited.

VENEERS

Veneers are thin sheets of exotic or decorative wood that are glued onto a groundwork of cheaper wood or manmade board which will not warp or split. Veneering is not a way of making a cheap job look more expensive. Some of the woods used as veneers are rare and expensive, and in some cases the trees themselves are very small or the wood itself is unstable. For these reasons, the woods are not used to make furniture. Occasionally, veneers are let into solid wood in the form of motifs, inlays, or strings – this is obviously a

skillful business and requires a great deal of patience. Over the years, veneer-cutting machinery has improved, and veneers have become ever thinner.

Hand Tools

Even the most basic repairs to furniture demand the use of a few tools. Some wood-working tools are highly specialized and are worth buying only if they are applicable to the particular job you are planning. Others can be used in a variety of different projects, and are therefore worth buying at the outset.

ESSENTIAL TOOLS

Discussed here are some of the basic tools you will need. The list could be expanded, and your collection of tools will grow as you gain in confidence and experience.

Screwdrivers are a necessity. It is as well to have a selection of both types, that is, crosshead and flathead.

Saws come in several shapes and sizes. The most useful are a small tenon saw, a coping saw, and a panel saw.

Hammers are necessary for tapping home nails and pins. Start with a medium-sized clawhammer and a pin hammer.

An awl looks like a small screwdriver but is in fact designed to start small holes for screws. It is an invaluable gadget.

Chisels are expensive, so choose your first set carefully. Bevel-edged chisels are the best type to opt for as they can be worked in tight corners. Firmer chisels are the alternative, but they are not so versatile.

Clamps (or cramps) are crucial to the cabinetmaker and restorer. In the short run, it is often cheaper to hire, rather than buy, sash clamps, but it is certainly worth purchasing a selection of G-clamps. Web or tourniquet clamps are inexpensive and are useful for holding entire pieces together.

A steel measuring tape and a boxwood rule are used in nearly every job. A square about 12in (30cm) long is a valuable instrument, as is a marking gauge.

A wheelbrace drill is needed for many jobs. The alternative is a brace, but braces are not so accurate, and their use demands more skill.

Planes come in many forms. A smoothing plane is the best type to start off with. For further discussion of planes, see page 15.

Among the miscellaneous tools you will need are sanding blocks, pliers, pincers, a sharpening stone, and a rasp or planer file.

Top (left to right)
Marking gauges, Bevel, Try squares (square), Conbination set and Carpentwrs pencils..

Middle
A selection of Wheelbraces and hand drills..

Left (top to bottom)
Awls, Bradawls, Grimltet and a Tacklifter.

Left (top to bottom)
Jack plane, Block planes, Smooth plane and a Spokeshove.

Left
Mallets

BUYING TOOLS
Always buy the best-quality tools you can afford and be particularly wary of plastic and imported tools – they do not wear well.

Electric and Special Tools

ELECTRIC TOOLS

Traditional cabinetmakers tend to twitch at the very mention of electric tools. However, used in moderation, they can make a job quicker and they take out some of the hard work. Mentioned here are some electric tools that can save you time and effort.

The electric drill is one of the most versatile and universally used tools. If you can afford it, choose a type that has variable speeds and that can be fitted with attachments.

An electric planer will remove enormous amounts of wood very quickly.

An electric router is handy for cutting rebates. The more sophisticated types can be adapted to cut dovetails.

A jigsaw is useful for cutting curved shapes out of sheet materials.

An orbital sander will make light work of rough surfaces. A belt sander is even more efficient.

Electric Tools

1 Electric drill
2 Router
3 Electric Planer
4 Cordless screwdriver
5 Heatgun
6 Jigsaw
7 Power saw (circular saw)

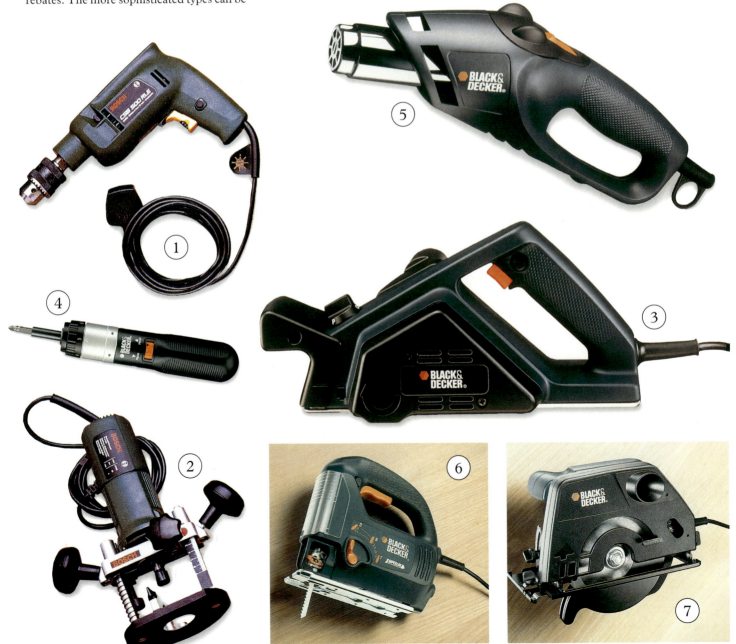

SPECIAL TOOLS

Some restoration work on wooden furniture demands the use of special tools. Of the many available, you may require some of the ones mentioned here.

There are various different types of planes. A shoulder plane is designed to cut across the grain of the wood. A multi-plane, or combination plane, is used for shaping moldings. Rebate planes can be fitted with different blades; they are designed to cut grooves and rebates in high-quality furniture.

The spokeshave is valuable for many tasks. There are several different types of blade and they can be adapted to shape pieces of wood to suit particular needs. Scraper planes are similar to spokeshaves but are used to remove varnish and paint, rather than wood.

Finally, the cabinet scraper is used to finish timber preparatory to painting or varnishing.

Special Tools

1 Rabbet plane
2 Compass plane
3 Router
4 Carving chisels (carving gouges)
5 Dovetail saw
6 Callipers

11 *An electric jigsaw makes light work of cutting out shapes.*

12 *Use a spokeshave to tidy up the rough edges left behind by the jigsaw.*

15 *By fitting a different blade in a router you can cut decorative grooves.*

16 *Before assembling the dresser, sand down all the end grains of the boards.*

17 Round off sharp corners on the visible edges of the boards with a plane.

18 Wrap sandpaper around a block before smoothing the boards.

19 Fix the shelf supports with nails and glue. Sink the nailheads below the surface. A filler of colored wax will help disguise any scars.

20 Before tightening the clamps, check that the frame is square by measuring the diagonals.

21 Use oval nails to consolidate the joints. These nails are less likely to split the wood.

22 Punch the nailheads below the surface of the wood so that they are invisible. A colored or plain filler or wax stopping will disguise the hole before waxing or polishing.

24 *Before varnishing, mix up a stain to match the color of the closet.*

Other Materials

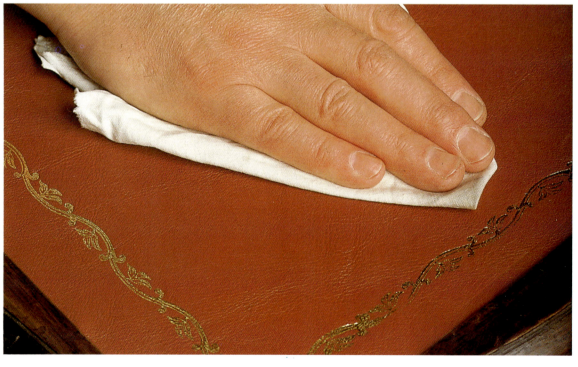

This section is devoted to the restoration of parts of furniture that are not made out of wood – materials from steel and plastic to *papier mâché* and cane are covered. Obviously, different skills and techniques are used on different materials but, by and large, anyone with any aptitude and a modest set of tools can tackle most of the repairs that he or she is likely to encounter.

Only a few of the repair and restoration techniques necessitate special equipment or materials, so provided that you have a reasonable work area you should have no trouble. One thing that is worth bearing in mind, however, is that certain chemicals and paints are potentially lethal if used in confined spaces. For this reason make sure that your workshop has adequate ventilation, especially if you are dealing with plastics. Do not take any risks.

As with any type of restoration work, skill comes with patience and practice, so do not expect a perfect result on your first attempt.

Top left
Repairing a corner on a
plastic drawer.
Bottom left
The finishing touches to the leather
of a relined wine table.
Top right
Replacing a glass panel in a
glazed bookcase.
Bottom right
Renewing a rush seat.

Metals and Plastics

Metal hinges, locks, and handles are found on all but the oldest and simplest furniture. Tough as most metals are, the passage of time means that wear and damage are inevitable. Directly replacing damaged metal parts would seem to be the easiest way of tackling a problem of this kind, but, in fact, although the commonest patterns of antique hardware are readily available, many of the less usual types of fittings are difficult to find. For this reason some skill at hardware repair is essential for the keen restorer.

Plastics of one sort or another are found in many different types of modern furniture and, because they are easily damaged, it makes sense to know how to repair them.

IDENTIFYING METALS

There are a half-dozen metals commonly found in furniture. Of these, iron and steel are the most used because they are strong and cheap. Steel, although it is often painted over as a protective measure, is silvery-gray in its natural state and may show signs of rust.

Brass is often used in inlays and to make small fittings, like hinges. It is relatively soft and should be handled with care. It is golden-yellow in color.

Bronze is usually brownish-pink, but it can be treated with chemicals to provide a green or a brown patina. It is a soft metal, and so is used mainly in decorative work.

Copper is a lovely metal; it is rose-pink when clean. Old copper often has a green patina, which can be toned down if necessary. Like bronze, copper is soft and should be treated with respect.

As a rule, aluminum is found only on modern furniture. It seldom corrodes, but it is surprisingly soft, and should be worked on with care.

Silver and gold are rarely found in solid form, but can often be found on antique furniture in the form of plating, to give the impression of greater opulence.

PLASTICS

There are literally hundreds of different plastics and they are not always easy to identify. Bakelite was one of the first plastics to be used in furniture construction; it is sometimes found used for drawer knobs. Unlike modern plastics, it does not burn easily.

Modern plastics – like acrylic sheeting, polystyrene, and polypropylene – melt at low temperatures, and this is often the reason why they need repair.

Nearly all plastics can be glued together, but make sure you use the right adhesive.

TOOLS

Metals and plastics can often be tackled with similar tools. For most repair jobs on these materials you should not need a wide range of equipment.

A fine-toothed hacksaw is essential for cutting both materials. A junior hacksaw is probably best for shaping plastics, whereas a large hacksaw is easier to use with metal.

An electric drill and a selection of high-speed (H.S.S.) drill bits are necessary to make holes, and fine files are handy for shaping.

JOINTING METHODS

Both metals and plastics can be molded and shaped, so jointing is not often required. However, there are many situations where two

or more pieces have to be joined together. There are several ways of doing this.

Sheets or plates of metal are sometimes riveted together. This can be satisfactory, but the rivets themselves can be something of an eyesore. If you want to rivet two pieces together, you will need a special riveting gun to do so.

A neater way of joining pieces of metal together is to use solder. To do this you need a soldering iron, wire solder, and flux (flux prevents the solder from oxidizing when it is being applied). Soldering does not provide a very strong join, but it can be perfectly adequate for small pieces.

When soldering, you should heat up the metals to be joined; using the tip of the soldering iron, apply the flux and then dab on the solder, which will melt. When the solder hardens, it will consolidate the join. Under no circumstances should you heat the solder directly with the iron – all you will create is a mess.

A third way of joining metals together is to weld them. This requires special tools and equipment and is usually beyond the scope of the amateur restorer.

Plastics are invariably glued together. Some adhesives melt the surfaces of the plastic, which then harden to give a neat and solid join. Most plastic adhesives are inflammable, so take the necessary precautions.

Tools for cutting metals

1 Fine files
2 Electric drill and metal drill bits
3 Electric Jig saw and selection of blades

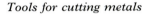

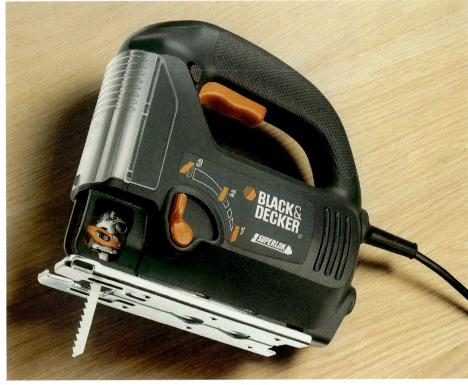

HANDLING METALS
AND PLASTICS
Take care when handling metals and plastics, especially if you are working with sheet materials.
Most metals, especially steel and iron, corrode easily. This can be exacerbated if fingerprints are left on the metal surfaces because fingerprints contain salts that promote rust. So after handling a metal always rub it down with an oily rag.
Plastics are relatively soft and are easily damaged. Acrylic sheeting is sold with a protective layer of paper stuck to it. Keep this paper in place for as long as possible because it prevents the surface from getting scratched.

Metal and Plastic Fittings

On these pages I have illustrated a few of the huge selection of metal and plastic fittings now available. Many fittings made for modern pieces of furniture are standardized, and you should have little trouble buying them at a D.I.Y. store. Old or antique fittings, however, are much more difficult to find. If you want to match such a fitting, the best way is to cannibalize a suitable, cheaply bought piece of second-hand furniture.

METAL FITTINGS

Among the most obvious metal fittings are locks, knobs, and hinges, which come in a range of styles and shapes.

Before buying or choosing a fitting, consider what metal you would prefer. Steel is robust, but it is not always very attractive, although you can get black-japanned or polished steels, both of which are easier on the eye. Brass often looks good, but, because it is not very strong, fittings made from it are necessarily simple in design. Needless to say, brass, copper, and bronze fittings are more expensive than their steel counterparts.

PLASTIC FITTINGS

Plastic fittings are often specially designed by manufacturers to suit specific products. For example, not all plastic kitchen drawers are the same; if you want a replacement drawer fitting you will almost certainly have to approach the manufacturer.

Plastic fittings, such as knobs and door handles, are often available not only in a variety of shapes and sizes but also in a range of colors. This is one of the great advantages of plastic over metal, especially if you are trying to coordinate a color scheme.

Right
Finding the right fittings for period furniture can be difficult. Sometimes you can adapt fittings bought from your local D.I.Y. store, but it is worth making a collection of any old fittings that come your way because they might come in useful in the future.

Far right
Do not be afraid of using plastic fittings. They often offer the best practical solution and nowadays they are both easy to fit and robust.

BRASS FITTINGS

PLASTIC FITTINGS

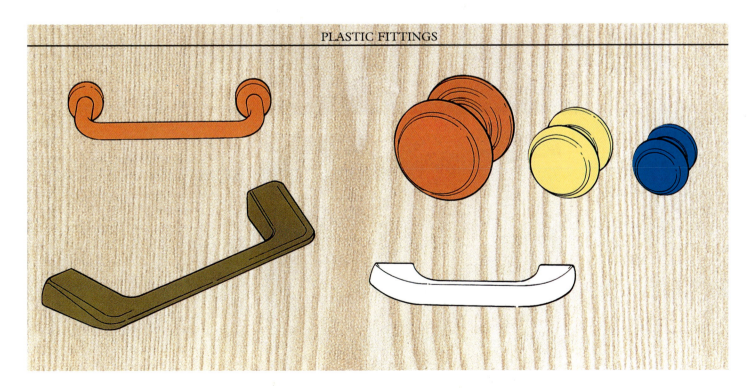

Metal Repairs

Although there is an infinite variety of things that can be constructed from metal, the same basic processes are employed in the making of most of them and, if you take your time, you should be able to produce creditable work. One thing that is not so easy to do is to dome or curve metal parts. Quite apart from the fact that you need special tools, considerable skill and practice are required. Always remember when working with metal that any rubbing of metal with metal produces heat, so allow time for the metal to cool before touching it.

MARKING OUT

If you want to cut out a replacement part, it is best first to make a template which you can use as a guide.

To make a good template, you need a sheet of stiff paper or card. Draw the outline you want on the card and then cut out the shape with a sharp knife or a pair of scissors.

Lay the template on the piece of metal you want to cut and scribe around it, using a hardened-steel point. Press down on the point with sufficient pressure to scratch the surface of the metal.

CUTTING METAL

Before attempting to cut a sheet of metal, make sure that it is securely anchored, as otherwise it will slide around, with the result that you will make a ragged cut. Cut thin sheet metal with a fine-toothed hacksaw, keeping the blade at a low angle so that the teeth do not catch on the edge. If you are tackling a thick sheet of metal, hold the blade at right angles to the workpiece.

FILING AND DRILLING METAL

The file is the metalworking equivalent of the woodworker's plane. It is used to shape metal and to take off unwanted burrs and edges. Files come in many shapes and types, but it is as well to use a good-quality one: cheap ones tend to become blunt very quickly. When using a file, hold both ends firmly and push it across the metal at an angle. Remember that a file cuts as you push it away from you.

There are a few golden rules when drilling metal. The first is to make sure that the piece is anchored, preferably in a special drill clamp. The second is to place an offcut of wood underneath the metal to protect the worktop and to support the workpiece as you drill through it. The third rule is to mark the hole with a center punch before you start drilling; if you fail to do this the drill bit may skid, which can damage the workpiece – as well as, of course, being extremely dangerous.

If you are using an electric drill, make sure that the speed is fast. Otherwise the bit may stick, which, again, can be dangerous. Also, ensure that you keep loose clothing and hair out of the way.

If you want to use bevel-headed screws to fix the sheet of metal in place, use a countersink bit to cut away around the hole.

If you are drilling a thick piece of steel, you must keep the bit lubricated or else it will overheat. A mixture of oil and water is the best lubricant, and it should be applied liberally. Thick blocks of metal are best drilled in a drill stand. This practice will guarantee that the hole is straight and is essential if you are using a small bit – without a drill stand, a small bit is quite likely to snap in two.

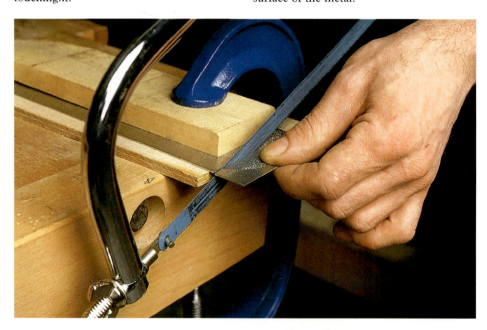

Sawing Metal

Above
Before sawing a thin sheet of metal, anchor it to the workbench with a G-clamp and sandwich it between two offcuts of wood. When sawing, keep the blade low.

Right
Stout bars of steel are best held firmly in a metalworker's vise. Saw with even strokes and do not apply too much pressure or the blade will stick.

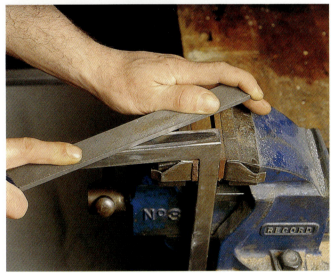

Filling Metal

Top

Clasp the workpiece firmly in a vise, using two offcuts to provide protection and support. Hold both ends of the file and work it across at an angle.

Above right

Strong pieces of metal do not have to be supported with offcuts, but they should be clamped in a vise.

Above

Remove burrs and sharp edges with a file. Do this with a minimum amount of pressure or there is a chance that you may scar the workpiece.

Drilling Metal

Right

Before drilling metal, mark the hole with a center punch – this will prevent the bit from skidding. Also, anchor the workpiece firmly to the workbench.

Far right

When drilling thick bars or sheets of metal, lubricate the drill bit with a mixture of oil and water. This will stop the bit from getting too hot.

Plastic Repairs

Plastic furniture is often best repaired using an appropriate adhesive (see pages 93-94), but you may have to cut and shape an insert before you can complete the repair. Most plastics are easy to saw and drill, using a combination of woodwork and metalwork tools. Always remember that plastics are easy to scratch and disfigure, so treat them carefully.

MAKING A TEMPLATE

As with any kind of insert repair, it is as well to make a template before you start cutting and shaping. In many cases, a paper template is more useful than a card one because it can be manipulated around curves if necessary.

After you have shaped your template, transfer the image to the sheet of plastic. If you are dealing with acrylic sheeting, leave the protective covering in place and mark the outline of the template onto it. Leave the protective covering in place for as long as possible.

CUTTING AND DRILLING PLASTICS

Most plastics can be sawn by hand, using a fine-toothed saw. It is not advisable to cut plastic with an electric jigsaw or circular saw because the speed of the blade is such that the frictional heat may melt the plastic, causing the edges to weld back together again even as the cut is being made. If you are cutting acrylic sheeting, lubricate the blade of your hacksaw with soapy water.

If rough edges are left behind after you have cut out the plastic smooth them down with fine wet-and-dry paper.

Plastics are easy to drill using standard high-speed (H.S.S.) bits. Always make sure that the workpiece is secure before you start drilling. If you are using an electric drill, be sure to wear goggles because some plastics are brittle and tiny chips may fly off. For similar reasons, it is a good idea to wear gloves as well.

REPAIRS TO REINFORCED PLASTICS

Some furniture is made from glass-reinforced polyester (G.R.P.) or glass-reinforced epoxy resin. Although these materials are very strong, they are also brittle and occasionally need repairing.

The best way of repairing these plastics is to use the contents of a car-repair kit.

Methods of repair vary, and it is always best to follow the manufacturer's instructions ,but with most types layers of fiberglass matting are fixed with an epoxy resin. When using these materials, be sure to protect yourself: they are toxic and give off dangerous fumes. Always wear gloves and, if required, a mask, and work in a well-ventilated room.

If necessary, you can touch up minor dents and superficial damage with an epoxy filler. With these fillers, the two parts are mixed up in the recommended proportions before they are applied to the surface. When the filler has set it can be sanded down flush with the surrounding surface and then painted.

Right
Most plastics can be cut with a fine-toothed saw. Hold the piece steady and saw slowly with firm, even strokes.

Below
Straight edges can be planed down. Hold the workpiece firm in a vise as you work the plane along the edge.

DEALING WITH SCRATCHES
Some plastics are notoriously easy to scratch, and most attempts to restore the surface only make matters worse. Toothpaste, which is a mild abrasive, can be very efficacious in removing scratches from hard plastics.

Above
To finish off a straight edge, clamp a sheet of wet-and-dry paper and a square block to the workbench. Run the edge of the plastic over the wet-and-dry paper while holding it tight against the block. Before drilling a piece of plastic, anchor it to the workbench. Drill slowly and wear protective goggles.

REPAIRS TO BROKEN DRAWERS

Drawers made from extruded plastic are found in many kitchens and bedrooms. These drawers are built from hollow, plastic strips, with all the necessary grooves and structural details molded in place. The strips are joined at the corners by plastic blocks that are usually glued or snapped into place. Damage to such drawers usually arises because they have been overloaded.

Repairs can often be effected by regluing the joints. If you have to reglue all the joints in a drawer, make sure that until the adhesive dries the drawer is held square by means of clamps.

Not all plastic drawers need adhesive for their repair: with some types a replacement piece can simply be snapped into place.

REPAIRING PLASTIC DRAWERS
Below left
Some plastic drawers, or drawers finished with plastic, are jointed at the corners with dowels. If these come loose, replace them and reassemble the drawer using fresh adhesive.
Below right
The corners on some drawers are jointed with sections of extruded plastic. With some types weak joints can be strengthened with adhesive. With others, you will have to get a new section that snaps into place.

Bending and Gluing Plastics

In order to make certain repairs to plastic furniture, you have to bend a new insert to fit. Bending rigid plastic is not difficult provided you heat it first and provided you make the curve or angle around a former. Most formers can be improvised from what is to hand - for example, the straight edge of a table or workbench is often perfectly adequate for shaping a right-angled corner.

Thin plastics can sometimes be heated with a hair-dryer until they are sufficiently malleable to be bent. Thicker plastics usually require more specifically applied heat. Assuming you want to bend a sheet of plastic into a right angle, your first task should be to mask off a line about ½in (12mm) wide. The best material to use for masking is cooking foil, as this reflects heat.

Hold the strips of foil in place with masking tape and then play a hair-dryer over the unmasked line. When the plastic starts to become supple, remove the heat and, as quickly as possible, shape the plastic over the former. If the heat from a hair-dryer is not strong enough to affect the plastic, hold the exposed line in front of a radiator. Remember, do not hold the plastic too close to the radiator as many plastics are inflammable.

If you do not want to try your hand at bending plastic, the obvious alternative is to join two pieces together with adhesive. In many respects this is the easier option.

1 Special adhesive is required to join sheets of acrylic together.

GLUING PLASTIC

1 Before gluing one sheet of plastic to another, clean up the edges using a flat sheet of fine wet-and-dry paper.

2 Mark a guideline where you want to attach the piece. Use a sharp implement held against a steel straight edge.

3 Apply adhesive along the edge to be fixed, making sure that you do not squeeze out too much.

4 Position the piece, and use a square to check that it is at right angles. Hold the piece in place until the adhesive sets.

4 Position the two pieces together and allow the adhesive to set. Remove excess adhesive with fine wet-and-dry paper.

GLUING ACRYLIC SHEETING

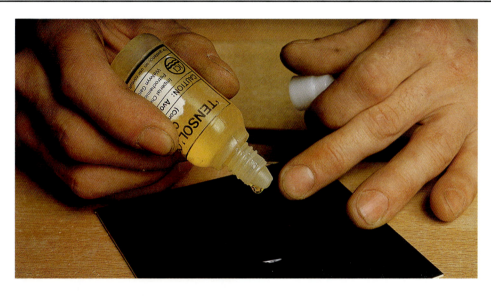

2 Pour out some of the adhesive onto a mixing board. Card is a good choice, because it will not react with the adhesive.

3 Apply the adhesive along one edge, using a pencil or a strip of wood as a tool. Spread the adhesive on sparingly.

5 Polish off dirt and dust with a soft, clean cloth. If you want to remove scratches, try using toothpaste as an abrasive.

6 If you want to reinforce the joint, drill a series of tiny holes through the repair.

7 Cut thin steel pins into short lengths and dip them into the adhesive. Then push the pins into the predrilled holes, using pliers.

Leather and Paper Linings

Leather covers have been used to protect table- and desktops for centuries. The glazed leather used is impervious to wine stains and ink blots, but it is soft and can quite easily be torn or otherwise damaged. Replacing a damaged leather covering is straightforward – but it is important to use specially prepared leather, which is available in a number of colors. Prepared leather has a uniform thickness and is supple and soft; the upper surface is glazed to add protection.

To replace the leather on a tabletop, you need a steel straight edge and a sharp, handyman's knife. The leather can be stuck in place with a starch-based decorating adhesive.

CLOTH LININGS

The cloth trim found in some drawers and chests serves to protect the contents of the drawer from unplaned wood. Cloth trims are easily torn and they are also susceptible to stains, but luckily it is not difficult to fit replacements. All you have to do is strip away the old cloth and tack or glue new trims in place.

Strip away old cloth by moistening it with warm water – this loosens the adhesive underneath. A flexible stripping knife is a handy tool to have to hand, especially if the fibers of the cloth have started to rot and decay. After stripping off the cloth, sand down the wood underneath until it is flat and even; do not forget the corners, which are where most of the glue will accumulate.

Linen is probably the best cloth to use as a replacement as it is both soft and strong. Cut it into suitably sized strips with a sharp pair of scissors and stick it in place with a diluted P.V.A. adhesive. Turn over the edges of the cloth before you smooth it down with a soft cloth or sponge.

PAPER LININGS

Paper linings were often used instead of cloth. These linings are often very beautiful, but they are fragile and can split and mark easily. Unless the piece is an expensive antique the best course of action is to replace the paper lining.

Strip off the old lining with a flexible scraper and a little warm water. Do not flood the paper with water as this can lead to swelling, cracks, and loose joints.

When the old paper has been stripped off, air the drawer or chest in a dry room for a couple of days or so.

Paper for relining work can often be found in interior-design stores. Lining paper traditionally used to be marbled, which is something you can do yourself (see below).

Laying in the new paper is simple enough. Use good scissors to trim each piece to size. Try to have as few joints as possible and attempt to match the pattern. Try the strips for size and, when you are satisfied, paste the inside of the box with lightweight wallpaper paste. Smooth down the paper with a clean, damp cloth or sponge.

1 Peel off the old lining in strips; it should come away easily. Sand down the surface to get rid of lumps and bumps and blobs of old glue.

5 Using a sharp knife held against a steel rule, cut the leather to fit. Try to avoid having to repeat cutting strokes.

CLEANING LEATHER AND CLOTH
Brittle and stained old leather can be cleaned with saddle soap. This is readily available from hardware and riding stores. Old cloth can be revived using a fabric shampoo. When applying the shampoo, try to keep the cloth as dry as possible; pat rather than rub the surface. Very fragile fabrics can be dry-cleaned, provided you sew them into a muslin bag first to protect them from the dry-cleaning machinery. Some old fabrics are now valuable, so it is always best to take advice before you attempt cleaning.

MARBLING PAPER
You can marble paper using enamel paints thinned to the consistency of milk. Put a few inches of water into a plastic bowl and divide the surface of the water in two with a strip of wood cut to fit. Pour three or more colors onto the water on one side of the stick and mix until the paints entwine. Pass a sheet of paper under the dividing stick from the clean water to the paint-covered side of the bowl. Draw the paper up through the paint, adjusting the speed so that you get the right effect. Hang the paper up to dry.

RELINING A WINE TABLE WITH LEATHER

2 Smear a thin layer of wallpaper adhesive over the tabletop. Leave this coat to dry and then apply a second.

3 When the second coat of adhesive becomes thick and tacky, lay on the new piece of leather, firming it into the corners as you work across the table.

4 Use a blunt kitchen knife to crease the leather along the edges of the rebate.

6 If you want to lay a gold pattern along the edge of the table, use gold leaf and a special gilding wheel (see pages 98-99).

7 Finally, clean up any excess adhesive and run over the leather with a clean cloth. To preserve the quality of the leather, treat it with saddle soap from time to time – this will keep it supple and smooth.

Gilding

Gilding is the art of decorating with gold. It is found mainly on fancy moldings, especially those surrounding elaborate picture and mirror frames. Traditional gilding was laid on gesso, a kind of pigmented plaster. The gesso was built up into shapes and forms and the gold was laid on top. Today it is comparatively simple to touch up damaged gilding, thanks to the large number of gold paints and pastes that are usually mixed with an oil – or wax-based binding. You can even get gilding sticks that work rather like a wax crayon. Of course, few of these touch-up materials contain real gold, but if you want to go the whole hog, you can always use gold leaf. Paints and pastes are usually rubbed or brushed on; some types demand that the surface be primed with size before application. Gold leaf is usually sold in sheets only a few microns thick, so it is very delicate and difficult to handle. It is commonly sold with a backing paper which protects it from damage. Although it is thin, gold leaf is far from transparent. In fact, it adds a touch of elegance and finesse which no other material can match. Gold leaf should be pressed or burnished onto a surface that has first been primed with size.

USING GOLD LEAF

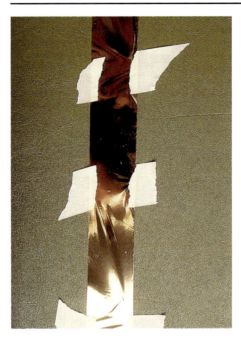

1 Gold leaf is ideal for laying down on soft surfaces like leather where no sizing is required. To lay down a decorative edging, tape down a strip of gold leaf. Try to keep it as flat as possible.

2 Run along the gold leaf with a heated gilding roller. Press down firmly and make sure you move the wheel along a straight line. A straight-edge board is useful as a guide.

GILDING WITH A GOLD STICK
Touch up chipped or flaking gilding by rubbing the stick over the damaged area. The surface should be clean, dry and grease-free before you start. Some gilding materials demand that the surface be primed with size first.

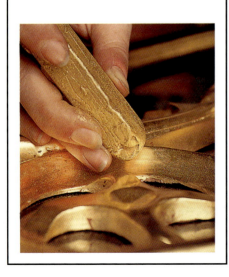

3 Gently lift up the strip of leaf. If you have pressed firmly enough the roller will have embossed the leaf into the surface.

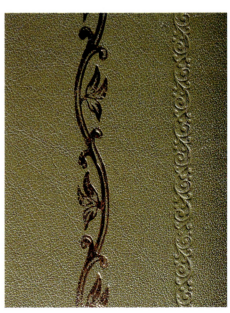

4 The finished effect. A variety of roller patterns are available.

USING TRANSFER LEAF

1 Coat the surface where the repair is to be made with red-oxide primer and sand very smooth. Brush a thin coat of gold size over the primed area and set aside.

2 Transfer leaf is gold leaf on a wax-paper backing. Half an hour after sizing the gilding can be done. Press the leaf gently onto the tacky surface.

3 Use a clean camel-hair brush to pat the gold leaf down against the sticky size. Use fragments of leaf to fill gaps in the coverage.

4 Burnish gently with a pad of cotton wool until the leaf adheres completely. Dip into a little spirit to remove smears.

Glass

Most modern glass is made on a float-glass production line. This gives a product which has little character or texture and which tends to look out of place with antique furniture. For this reason, take great care when handling old glass – buying a suitable replacement piece may prove difficult.

There are several types of glass, so if you plan to replace a broken pane in a bookcase, for example, look around until you find the exact sort you want. Specialist glaziers are more likely to have what you require than a local hardware or D.I.Y. store.

TYPES OF GLASS
Different types of glass can vary considerably in quality and strength and so it is worth knowing something about the commonest sorts before you go out and buy.

Sheet glass is quite difficult to buy in small quantities. It is usually thin – ⅛in (3mm) or less – and it is sometimes suitable for use in old furniture. This is because it has ripples and flaws that give it character.

Float glass comes in a range of thicknesses: from a little over ⅛in (4mm) up to 1in (25mm). Glass ⅜in (9mm) thick is commonly found in windows, but glass for tabletops and shelves usually varies in thickness between ⅜in (9mm) and ⅝in (15mm).

Diffuse-reflection glass has microscopic dimples in its surface and these reduce reflections from nearby light sources. This type of glass is often used in picture-framing.

Patterned glass is available in hundreds of different designs and in various thicknesses. However, it is not always easy to find a matching replacement.

Spun glass is difficult to find, but some Arts & Crafts furniture requires the

ornamental centers for decoration. It can be obtained from specialist suppliers.

TOOLS
The most essential tool for glazing is a decent glass-cutter. There are several different types, but a wheel-cutter is as good a choice as any.

To drill glass, you need a special bit with a tungsten tip. These are always used with a lubricant, such as light engineering oil, as they can get very hot in use.

A pair of pliers and a putty knife are necessary if you are replacing a broken pane.

HANDLING GLASS
Always wear gloves when handling sheets of glass. Thin leather ones are ideal – thick ones tend to be clumsy.

When you carry glass, always hold it under one arm; big sheets are best carried by two people – one at each end.

Glass is not easy to cut cleanly, nor is it easy to drill. Life is made much easier if you can provide a bed for the sheet of glass that you are working on. Thick felt is ideal, but using several layers of newspaper works equally well.

If you want to grind down the edges of a sheet of glass, you would be well advised to have this done professionally. Grinding glass is a skillful business and the cost of having the edges ground for you is well worth it. However, if you just want to round off sharp edges, try running a wet carborundum stone along them.

1 Wheel glass-cutter
2 Tungsten-tipped spearpoint glass drill bit
3 Glazier's putty knife
4 Glazier's plier

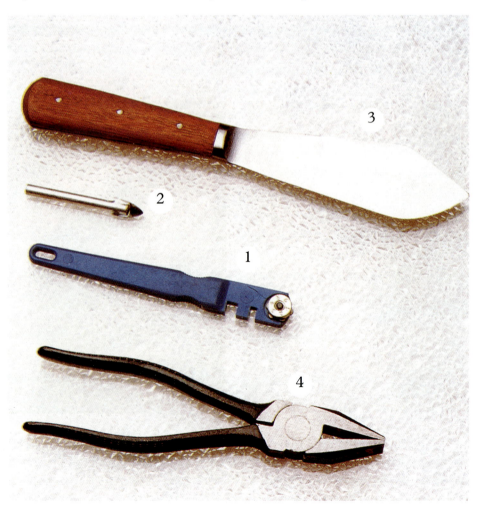

SAFETY
In many countries there are strict laws about the type of glass that can be used for windows, doors, and tabletops. It is wise to check before you buy. Your local glazier should be able to advise you on these laws. Never forget that glass can be extremely dangerous and it is always best to play safe, especially if there are children around the house.

REPAIRING A GLAZED BOOKCASE

1 *Remove any fragments of broken glass from the rebate and then make a card template.*

2 *Lay a sheet of glass on a bed of newspapers and, holding the glass-cutter like a pen against a straight edge, score the glass. Slip* the straight edge under the score and press down on the glass to snap it.

3 *If you want to cut out a curve you will have to score a line freehand.*

4 *Mix a compatible stain in with the glazier's putty to match the color of the wood. The putty must be free of lumps.*

5 *Line the rebate with putty, rolling it out with your thumb.*

6 *Push the new pane into the putty and rub off any excess with a finer. On the front of the panel, bevel the putty using a putty knife.*

Mirrors and Leaded Lights

Repairs to damaged mirrors and leaded lights are different from other glass repairs, both because the glass is especially prepared and because it is fixed in a unique way.

MIRRORS

Modern mirrors are generally made from flat glass whose rear has been sprayed with a thin coating of silver. They give a near-perfect reflection, although it is common to find that the reflective coating has been scratched or has started to corrode. Old mirrors, on the other hand, were often coated with a thin deposit of a mercury-tin amalgam. This gives a soft and slightly greenish cast to the reflection.

On the whole, it is best to avoid trying to touch up a damaged reflective surface. For one thing, the chemicals used are often toxic and contain substances like mercury, arsenic, and lead. If you want to have a mirror re-silvered, ask your local glazier, who should be able to help or give advice. It should be remembered that very old glass should be re-silvered only after you have taken expert advice, since the repair may reduce the value of the piece to collectors.

LEADED LIGHTS

Leaded lights are made up of regular or fancy-shaped panes of glass held together by strips of lead whose cross-section looks like an "H." This was the traditional method of making windows from small, handmade panes of glass. Individual panes can be replaced quite easily, although you may have to improvise a few tools.

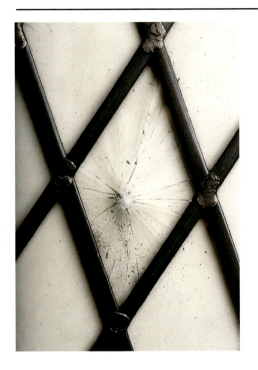

1 *Although it may appear to be difficult to replace a broken pane in a leaded light, the job is surprisingly easy.*

Left

Typical of the color and condition of old mirrors is this fragment laid on an elaborate, reproduction mirror. Note that the softer color of old mirrors has been achieved in the reproduction by choosing one of the variety of modern mirror finishes now available. An even more effective result can be obtained by chemically ageing the modern "silvering" – although this is a specialist job.

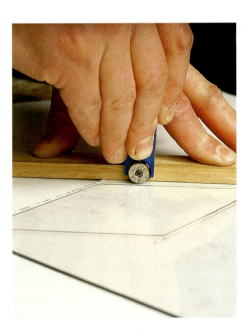

5 *Add the depth of the rebate to your drawing and then cut out a pane to fit. Use a straight edge as a guide, and press down firmly on the cutter.*

Dovetail joint
A joint formed by one or more tapering projections (dovetails) on one board, fitted tightly into mortises carved into another.

Dowel
A round pin or peg used in jointing.

Dralon velvet
Imitation velvet made from Dralon, trade name for a fabric made from a mixture of cotton and synthetic fibers. Dralon velvet has the advantage that, unlike traditional velvet, it can be washed.

Drop-in seat
In a chair, a seat that has been constructed as a separate entity from the rest of the chair. Sometimes drop-in seats have been tacked in place, but often they can be simply removed by knocking them out.

Dual stone
An oilstone, having a rough texture on one side and a fine texture on the other.

English webbing
Webbing made from strips of fabric – unlike Pirelli webbing, which is made from strips of rubber.

Epoxy adhesives
Adhesives based on an epoxy (or epoxide) resin or several such resins. They are of limited use in cabinetmaking, but can come in useful for quick repairs.

Fadding
Laying on the first layer of French polish. Traditionally this is done with a burnisher, but most people find it easier to brush the French polish on.

Fillet
A strip of wood added to the work as either a guide or a support.

Float glass
A type of glass made by floating molten glass on a liquid of higher density so that it hardens into a flat sheet.

Fluteroni
A wide, U-shaped, carving gouge with round corners, used for shaping round sides.

Fore plane
A plane of length between those of the jack plane and the trying plane.

Frame saw
A saw with a narrow blade tensioned and supported in a wooden frame.

French polish
A solution of shellac in alcohol used to give furniture a shiny finish. The alcohol evaporates to leave a thin coating of shellac on the piece.

Fretsaw
A small saw that looks rather like a miniature hacksaw. It can be useful for cutting ornamental work or, in certain circumstances, for cutting holes in sheets of wood.

Furnishing fabric
A catch-all name covering chintzes, plain or patterned, heavy-duty fabrics and various manmade fabrics.

Garnet paper
One of the coarsest types of abrasive papers.

G-clamp or C-clamp
Used for small clamping work, these clamps get their names because of their shapes.

Gent's back saw
A small saw with a round handle and a thin blade, used for cutting dovetails and for other small work.

Gesso
A pigmented plaster which can be formed into a molding, as in a picture frame.

Gooseneck scraper
Named for its general appearance, this is a scraper that is invaluable for cleaning certain types of moldings and other shaped pieces of wood.

Grit size
A measure of the roughness of an abrasive paper. The lower the figure given for the grit size the coarser the paper.

Hacksaw
A saw used for cutting metals and plastics.

It has a thin, steel blade held in a U-shaped frame to which a handle is attached.

Hardwood
Wood from a deciduous tree.

Heartwood
The best timber. It comes from the heart of the tree and has matured with age.

Hessian
A plain-woven, coarse fabric made from jute or hemp.

Hickory
A whitish-yellow wood which is very tough, hard, elastic, and strong. It is widely used for the handles of hammers.

Hogging
The rough planing of timber, usually using a jack plane that has a slightly rounded cutter.

Honing guide
see sharpening guide

Inlay
A form of decoration where pieces of wood and other materials are set into a base of wood and rendered flush.

Jack plane
The most commonly used plane. It gets its name from the expression "Jack of all trades."

Jigsaw
A saw with a thin, steel blade which is used for cutting intricate curves.

Jointer
A long plane that is particularly useful when planing long boards.

Keying
An addition to a piece of wood, used to strengthen it. Dovetail keying is where the piece of wood is inserted into a dovetailed housing to prevent a board from warping.

Keyhole saw
A saw similar to the compass saw, having a thin, tapering blade. It is used for cutting keyholes and similar slots.

Leaded lights
Panes of glass held together with lead strips of an H-shaped cross-section. Leaded lights are frequently found in the windows of old houses or on the fronts of antique dressers.

Lengthening bar
An addition used with a sash clamp to give added capacity.

Log saw
A thin-bladed saw with a tubular frame used for logging and large, rough work.

Macaroni
A wide, U-shaped, carving gouge with square corners, designed for finishing the sides of shallow recesses.

Mahogany
A fairly hard, reddish-brown timber of many varieties. Mahogany is used both for furniture and as a base for veneering.

Marbling
Using paint or ink to create the appearance or general effect of variegated marble.

Marquetry
A pattern made of inlaid veneers of wood, ivory, metal, or other substance in order to form a picture or design. The word "marquetry" refers also to the art of making such pictures or designs.

M.D.F. (Mass-density fiberboard)
A manmade board used in mainly in making kitchen and bathroom cabinets. It has limited uses in furniture restoration.

Miter
A joint formed by cutting the edges of two pieces of timber at an equal angle – usually 45°.

Miter square
A tool used to test and mark lines at an angle of 45°.

Mortise
A usually rectangular slot or recess cut into a piece of timber and designed to receive a male part, or tenon.

Mortise chisel or registered pattern
A strong chisel specially designed for

cutting mortises. It has a thicker blade than the standard, plus a steel hoop and ferrule to hold the blade securely in the handle and protect the handle from splitting.

Moldings or beadings
Pieces of timber with a preshaped profile, used for the edgings of furniture.

Multiplane or combination plane
A plane capable of plowing, rebating, beading, and tonguing.

Oilstone
A fine-grained stone, lubricated with oil, which is used for sharpening cutting edges.

Oilstone slip
A shaped oilstone which is used for sharpening gouges.

Overstuffing
A technique frequently used in the construction of upholstered chairs. The springs are attached to the webbing, covered with fiber and held down by a coarse covering; then a further layer of stuffing is added before the final hessian covering.

Palm plane
A small plane which fits comfortably into the hand. It is useful when dealing with smaller, intricate work.

Parquetry
A geometric pattern constructed from inlaid pieces of wood, often of different textures and colors. Parquetry is most frequently employed in flooring.

Pearls
The granules in which animal glue is sometimes supplied.

Piano hinge
Essentially a butt hinge, but with leaves that are considerably longer.

Pirelli webbing
Webbing made from strips of rubber rather than from fabric.

Plinth
The receding part of a cabinet next to the floor.

Plow
A plane for making grooves or rebates.

P.V.A. (or white woodworker's adhesive)
A frequently used adhesive which has as its base a synthetic resin called polyvinyl acetate.

Quick gouge
A deep-carving gouge for roughing-out.

Quilted tapestry
Tapestry woven in two layers to give a heavy, embossed appearance.

Rabbet
see rebate

Rail
The horizontal member of a frame.

Rebate or rabbet
A cut made on the edge of a frame or board to receive a sheet of glass or a wooden panel.

Rebate plane
A plane which can be fitted with different blades, used to cut grooves and rebates in high-quality furniture.

Registered pattern
see mortise chisel

Rip saw
A saw with special teeth designed for use when cutting with the grain.

Rosewood
A beautiful, dark, purplish-brown-colored wood used for expensive cabinetwork, tool handles, and other components.

Router
A hand or machine tool used to make a variety of cuts.

Sash clamp
Large clamp used to hold major components of furniture.

Sawhorse
A stand used to hold wood while it is being sawed. It is now possible to buy manufactured sawhorses which also feature

vices and other ancillary gadgets.

Saw set
A pincer-like tool that is used for setting saw teeth.

Scraper plane
A device rather like a spokeshave, but used to remove varnish and paint rather than wood.

Scratchstock
A small too! used to cut shallow recesses for inlaying.

Scrim
Open-weave cotton or linen fabric used for curtains, drapes etc.

Set
The inclination of alternate teeth of a saw from left to right. The term is used also for the distance that the cap iron is set back from the cutting edge of a plane.

Sharpening guide (or honing guide)
A device used when sharpening the blades of chisels or planes. It holds the blade against the oilstone at the correct angle.

Sheet glass
A type of glass made in cylindrical form and then flattened out. It is of interest to the furniture-maker because it has flaws and therefore character.

Shoulder plane
A precision plane which cuts across the grain to trim end grain before jointing.

Silicon-carbide paper
see wet-and-dry paper

Skew chisel
A chisel used for planing wood between lathe centers, squaring, beading, curving, and tapering.

Slow gouge
A shallow-carving gouge for finishing work.

Softwood
Wood from a coniferous tree.

Spokeshave
A cutting tool with two handles, used for small, curved work. Its effect is similar to

that of a plane.

Strings
Tiny strips of thin wood, square or rectangular in cross-section, used in inlaying.

Synthetic-resin adhesives
Adhesives based on synthetic resins which are supplied in two parts - a thick, syrupy liquid and a hardener.

Tapestry
A heavy, ornamental fabric.

Tenon
The male part of a mortise joint.

Toothing
The roughing-up of the surface of wood in order to provide keying for veneers.

Trying plane
A long, bench plane used in the same way and for the same purposes as a jointer.

Tungsten-carbide grit
The ultimate in manmade, abrasive grits, used for abrasive papers and wheels.

Tweed
A coarse, wool fabric, woven usually in two or more colors.

Uraldehyde glues
A type of slow-setting adhesive that is very useful in furniture repairing.

Valance
A short curtain of drapery hung along a piece of furniture both for decoration and to hide structural detail.

Velcro
Trade name for a type of fastening made of two nylon strips. One has a coarse surface, whereas the other is made up of countless tiny hooks, so that when the two surfaces are pushed together they form a bond which is strong but can nevertheless easily be ripped open whenever desired.

Veneer
Thin piece of wood glued to a solid timber background for the purposes of decoration. This allows you to use rare and exotic woods which either are not available in

solid form or would be too expensive.

Veneering hammer
A tool used when gluing veneers to flatten them down and assist the joining.

Veneer punch
A punch used in making repairs to veneers.

Veiner
A tiny, deep, U-shaped gouge used in texturing and veining.

Vise
A device, usually featuring a pair of jaws, designed to hold wood or other material while work is being done on it.

Warping
The twisting of timber as it dries.

Wax polish
A polish, used on furniture, which contains various synthetic waxes, as well as, if of highest-quality, natural beeswax.

Webbing
Strong, fabric strips of hemp, cotton, jute, or rubber used as a support under springs.

Wet-and-dry paper
A type of abrasive paper that can be used wet. The grit is silicon carbide, and the paper and glue are waterproof.

White woodworker's adhesive
see P.V.A.

INDEX

INDEX 173

G

ACKNOWLEDGEMENTS

DEMONSTRATION CREDITS
Leslie Charteris
Malcolm Hopkins
Leslie Howes
Sarah Nagy
Mark Treasure

EQUIPMENT CREDITS
Pages : Draper tools Ltd.,Black & Decker,
Buck and Ryan, J D Beardmore, Mr Price.
S Tysacks, Bellenger and Price Ltd.

Special thanks to Bob Cocker, Jan Orchard,
and Paul Forrester.

PICTURE CREDITS
Page 11, top right: M. Dunne, Elizabeth
Whiting and Associates; page 65, bottom left:
Tim Street Porter, Elizabeth Whiting and
Associates; page 91, bottom right: Maddox;
pages 105 and 112, cane and *papier-mâché*
chairs: Karin Craddock; page 180, top left:
M. Dunne, Elizabeth Whiting and Associates.

While every effort has been made to ensure
that the information in this book is correct at
the time of going to press, the publisher cannot
accept responsibility for any inaccuracies.